RunSmart

•

Running for local office on a shoestring

Ken Maddox   Michael Richman

iUniverse, Inc.
New York   Bloomington

RunSmart
Running for local office on a shoestring

iUniverse books may be ordered through booksellers or by contacting:

iUniverse
1663 Liberty Drive
Bloomington, IN 47403
www.iuniverse.com
1-800-Authors (1-800-288-4677)

ISBN: 978-0-595-47174-4 (pbk)
ISBN: 978-0-595-91454-8 (ebk)

Printed in the United States of America

Dedicated To The Memory Of
Martin Calhoun

Contents

Foreword

As a lifelong conservative activist, I've never chosen to run for public office. Instead, I've focused on the internal workings of the Republican Party and endeavored to get fellow conservatives elected, especially to local office.

The clear need to have quality people in office have time and time again proven to be true. I've always thought the government closest to the people is the most responsive to their needs. As such, they tend to be more accountable to the people they are elected to serve.

As much as I care about a candidate's political leanings, I am more concerned with their character. As a citizen, I want my elected officials to be good, decent people. I want them to listen to and care about the communities they serve.

I encourage you to run for local office or support someone who is. We are blessed to live in a nation where diversity of political thought is encouraged and people of all backgrounds can debate policy in the marketplace of ideas. Both political parties need good people serving in local government. City council and school board seats are where we find our next State Legislators and future members of Congress. Of course, always feel free to register as a Republican.

Shawn Steel
Past Chairman
California Republican Party

YOU CAN'T SEIZE THE INITIATIVE
IF YOU FAIL TO REALIZE YOU HAVE IT

Introduction

Okay, so here is your obligatory "Congratulations on your decision to run for local office" statement. Now, get over yourself. Hundreds of thousands of people throughout this country run for local office and lose. Winning requires a deep commitment. You must be willing to put in the hours required to walk precincts, raise money, and make voter contact. There truly is no prize for second place.

Mike and I decided to write this guide to run for local office because so much of what is out there is written by political scientists. Nothing against these learned professors but running for office, especially at the local level, requires a practical road map to victory. This is not a game of theory and musings over national or state direction. You need the nuts and bolts of how to put together a simple game plan that makes the most of the resources you have.

Most races for local office are conducted around the kitchen table on very little money. This book will serve as your guide. However, this book is not a text on how to write copy or any other of a myriad of topics we could probably go into great depth about. Our book is an overview of what you need to do to win. It is intended for those of you who have very little money with which to run a campaign.

We are going to explore the role of political parties even in local politics. You are going to learn about walk sheets, how to deal with vendors, different aspects of the media mix, and much more.

Getting on the Ballot

"Fortune favors the bold"

—Sun Tzu, The Art of War, 6ᵗʰ Century BC

Local offices

There are basically three types of local offices you can run for: city council, school board and special district. City council and school board are self explanatory, but what is a special district? These are "shadow governments" overseen by elected officials who often go unopposed. These can be water districts, fire protection districts, sanitation districts and even library districts.

Why would anyone want to serve on a special district? Some people want to serve because they have a true interest in the subject and want to improve the quality of service provided. For example, we have friends that serve on local water boards. The importance of water delivery and conservation are obvious. Those we know are experts on the subject. Others clutch onto these seats for the benefit package received as a member of their Board.

Local elected office won't earn you much in the way of a paycheck. However, the seat often comes with health benefits and the ability to gain time in a public employee retirement system. More importantly, there are the intangible rewards of being part of the governance of your community.

Go to a special district meeting and see how many senior citizens sit on them. You will also see food is served at every meeting. This doesn't mean they aren't interested in the subject. Many have become experts in their subject area. They also might be interested in the benefits of elected office. Many of those elected to a special district post go unchallenged and remain in those seats for a very long time.

Don't be afraid to run for one of these offices. You can use it to run for city council, school board or another office. But keep in mind, these offices are low profile and the incumbent has a very distinct advantage. You will need to raise the profile of the post and convince voters they need a change.

Biases

Be prepared for biases on the part of voters. These can work for or against you. There is usually a bias in favor of men for city council. This is due, in large part, to the nature of the issues in a city council race. The same holds true for women in school board races. Parents tend to have a favorable bias toward women when it comes to the education of their children.

Racial biases can also come into play. These tend to follow stereotypes.

You might be running for office in an ethnic community that is focused on seeing that someone of their racial background is elected.

The bottom line is voters are people with the same good and bad qualities, and preconceived notions and prejudices as the general public. Some of these biases can vary depending on the socioeconomic background of the community. Be prepared for them.

Candidate filing

City council candidates will typically file with their local election official. This is usually the city clerk. Nomination papers and economic disclosure statements and contribution disclosures will normally be filed with the city clerk who will provide copies to the Secretary of State.

School board candidates and all others will typically file with the Registrar of Voters in the county where they reside.

Nomination papers need to be signed by registered voters. Everyone will say they are registered even if they are not. Make sure you get extras in case some of your signatures are disqualified.

You can use the names on your walk sheets as a place to start. This way you know each one of them is registered. The role of walk sheets will be covered later.

Again, laws vary from state to state. But it is probably wise to allow the person signing your nomination papers to fill out their name and address themselves so the signature isn't disqualified.

There was a school board recall taking place in a Southern California school district. Multiple members of the Board were being recalled. Signature gatherers had voters sign all the sheets but in the interest of time had the voter only fill out their address on one. The signature gatherers then filled out the addresses on the remaining sheets. The Registrar of Voters disqualified the signatures despite the voter having had signed them all.

Make sure you know the laws in your area and get the rules in writing. Don't rely on verbal instructions from any government agency.

Economic disclosure

Laws differ from state to state and city to city but it is not unusual for candidates to file some type of economic disclosure indicating where the candidate earns their income. This helps to identity conflicts of interest. Penalties can be assessed for failure to file.

Campaign disclosure

You will most likely be required to file the appropriate forms with your elections official indicating where your contributions came from. You really need to understand the law with respect to who can give you money and how you report it.

Seminars are available from the regulatory body overseeing campaign finance law. Professional campaign treasurers are also available for hire. You can always call the headquarters of your political party and ask them for some names of campaign treasurers.

You will probably need to obtain a campaign identification number. In California, these are obtained from the Fair Political Practices Committee. The names and laws can vary from state to state.

Investigate these requirements thoroughly. You can be fined for not filing the paperwork correctly and on time, and your opponents may use the fact that you misfiled as a campaign issue, calling you irresponsible and not law abiding.

You as Candidate

"The wise are glad to be instructed, but babbling fools fall flat on their faces"

—*Proverbs 10:8, NLT Bible*

Know why you're a candidate

People run for office for a variety of reasons. These can include but are not limited to:

- Wanting To Make Their Community A Better Place—"The Good Government Candidate"

- Upset About A Singular Event In Their Community—"The Stop Sign Candidate"

- Upset About A Lack Of Leadership In Their Community—"The Activist"

- A Hunger For Politics And Wanting To Get Into The Mix—"Mr. or Ms. Ambition"

A host of candidates who have chosen to run for a local office that did so for any of the above reasons were successful. Let's take a look at each of these candidates.

The good government candidate

This is the person who genuinely wants to be involved and see their community improve. Typically, they aren't interested in ever running for higher office. They usually belong to a civic group of two. They might use a consultant to help them with their political campaign depending on their resources. Often, they sit around the kitchen table with supporters and come up with their strategy.

They also tend to be naive about what they are getting into. Some "good government" types evolve into "Mr. Ambition." We'll look at this further later on. These candidates tend not to be decisive for fear of not making everyone happy, and also are likely to become beholden to local special interests. The voters are already stuck with plenty of handwringers. Don't add to this already pervasive problem.

The stop sign candidate

You can find these types at virtually any council meeting. These are the people who can't just let go. They believe the issue they care about is the foremost issue in everybody else's world. They are narcissistic in a way. The entire community needs to revolve around what is important to them.

They are also deluded into thinking they can win with no money by talking about their pet issue. Their issues may be a stop sign that should or shouldn't exist. Maybe it is fireworks. Just about anything can qualify as the issue everyone should care about. A very popular current trend is, "No Growthers." These candidates only care about having the least amount of new housing and new commercial development.

Upset about a lack of leadership

These candidates tend to be activists. They can be very similar to the "good government" candidate but are by nature much more decisive. They tend to be involved in their community and just get fed up. Often they have to be coaxed into running for office. They are the revolutionaries who get called upon to govern and don't relish the idea.

Mr. or Ms. Ambition

These are the best candidates as long as they aren't crazy. Yes, this needed to be pointed out. Too often ambitious people in politics are, well, just plain off their rocker. Every elected official knows these types. They tend to be perennial candidates. Always looking for a seat they might be able to win. Seeking out a seat where you can be victorious is smart if you are a Mr. or Ms. Ambition, but someone other than you should think you should be in office. You can often find the crazy types running for the seats they can't win in partisan races. They tend to be sacrificial lambs who take one for the team. This way they get the attention they want with no disgrace if unsuccessful.

For the record, there are good political party activists who also take one for the team by running against a well-entrenched candidate of the other party. Once you get involved in party politics, you can easily distinguish between these two.

Ambitious candidates get over the natural inclination to avoid asking for money. "Money is the mother's milk of politics," said the longtime Speaker of the California State Assembly Jess Unruh. Almost no one likes asking for money, but do it long enough and you'll find yourself much more confident in all your abilities.

Ambitious candidates are willing to work. Yes, running for office is hard work. It involves organizing volunteers, walking precincts, fundraising, sending out press releases, and all those other duties as assigned. Typically, candidates for local office don't have much in the way of staff to help. Campaign staff usually consists of the candidate's spouse and one or two well-meaning friends.

Ambitious candidates are also often concerned with good government. Although, we have differentiated between "good government" candidates and "ambitious candidates" that doesn't mean a candidate with ambition can't also be concerned about providing good government to their prospective constituents.

Lastly, you need to be able to briefly articulate why you're running for office. Avoid overly negative talk about your opponent in this statement. People like their candidates to be positive. Yes, you will need to point to differences and highlight why you should be the officeholder and not the incumbent or one of your opponents. Don't try to put everything into the "why you are running" answer.

Try something tailored to your needs like this:

"I'm running for city council because I love our community. However, there have been missed opportunities to attract good paying jobs, improve our parks, and maintain the quality of life we all want."

Campaign Issues

"Wise speech is rarer and more valuable than gold and rubies"

—Proverbs 20:15, NLT Bible

What are the issues?

This may sting a bit but everyone else may not share your issues. Oh, so you asked your friends and they all agree with you. Well, then, it's settled. C'mon, most of us spend our time with like-minded individuals. Yes, I've seen candidates who identified the most important issues. You might be one of them. I only raise this as a point of caution.

I (Ken) recently ran the campaign for a candidate who was challenging an incumbent. The incumbent was appointed to fill a vacancy on the city council. He was active in many civic organizations. The most important issue for this candidate was fireworks. The city still allowed "safe and sane" fireworks and he wanted to ban them.

He believed virtually everyone in this city of roughly 170,000 people agreed with him. If he bothered to leave his home on July 4th, he would've learned otherwise. The city loves fireworks. The streets practically shut down with block parties.

A little research showed the same city had one of the highest number of sex offenders in the county. My candidate ran on a platform of working to rid the city of these sex offenders.

Imagine you are the voter. Would you be more concerned with ridding your city of "safe and sane" fireworks once a year or with information that 40 or so high risk sex offenders live in your ZIP code? Needless to say, my candidate trounced the incumbent.

There are traditional issues you can run for if there aren't definitive issues in your race.

City Council IssuesDevelopment

- Traffic

- Crime

- Jobs

- Taxes

School Board Issues

- Test Scores

- School Safety

- Educational Programs

- Pedagogy

Special Districts (Sanitation, Water etc.)

Taxes

Water Quality

Fiduciary Responsibility

Fundraising

"Pride precedes the man before the fall"

—Proverbs 16:18, NLT Bible

Fundraising strategy

Karl von Clauswitz is mandatory reading for U.S. Army officers. He was a great military Prussian military strategist. Many of his dictums can be applied to your race for political office.

Money is to be considered like a lubricant, which, by reducing all natural frictions, allows a much greater diversity and mobility of all forces.[1]

The easiest way to find out who gives money to candidates running for the office you're seeking is to obtain copies, which are available from your local clerk's office, of the campaign contributions of the incumbent members of the elected body.

However, it will be hard to raise money from these entities unless the incumbent members of the entity you're seeking to be elected to support you.

You're probably going to have to spend some of your own money. This can be mitigated by your "friends and family" letter asking for money. Hope they send you some. Your own money can be listed as a loan on your paperwork.

You will find it easier to raise money after you win. Money raised can be used to pay back loans to the campaign. However, we don't recommend taking loans from others during this step in your political career. You don't want to get sued for failure to pay the loans back.

Also, it's a good idea to get appointed to a community board of some kind. For example, a person running for city council has an advantage if they serve on the planning commission. Lesser commissions such as traffic and parks can also help.

A planning commissioner can raise money from interests in the city with projects submitted. We can already hear you bright eyed neophytes saying, 'How can that be? Isn't this a conflict?' No! It's only a conflict if you're personally enriched by your decision.

Commission titles can also be helpful as part of a ballot designation. This will be covered in more detail later.

School board candidates have an even tougher time raising money. After all, few persons have an interest in their school board beyond that of the student's parents. Only the most active PTA or PTO members would be interested enough to donate money with the exception of vendors who do business with the district. However, vendors are going to be hard pressed to spend money against an incumbent.

---

1   Clauswitz, Karl von. *On War.* 1832.

School board candidates typically receive their contributions from employee bargaining groups consisting of the faculty and classified personnel.

Builders might be interested in giving money if a bond measure has recently been passed, meaning school construction contracts will soon be awarded.

Special district candidates face many of the same problems as school board candidates. Who lies awake at night worrying who will be elected to a water board? Employee bargaining units might also be involved in a race of this type.

Many public works projects have been performed by contractors who pay prevailing wages. This means union labor. Expect the "trades" to financially support candidates favorable to their position when major construction projects are soon underway.

Waste not want not

Don't spend more money on the fundraiser than you take in. This might sound simple but I've seen many candidates try to attract donors by putting on an expensive event. People donate because they either like you and agree with your platform, think you are going to win and will want something from you, or can't stand your opponent. Donors don't come for the food and drinks.

There have been many successful fundraisers that provided nothing more than coffee and cookies for refreshments.

A restaurant or hotel will ask you if you want a hosted or no hosted bar. Your answer should be no host. You might want to limit complimentary beverages to soft drinks and coffee. Keep the food simple.

Your invitations should also be created on the cheap. You aren't inviting people to a wedding. You'll probably need to include your campaign identification number on your materials. Check with your local elections officer for the information that by law needs to be included on your materials.

Before the invitations go out you might be able to get sponsors. Ask those already elected to serve on the "host committee." This will give you credibility with existing donors. An invitation to a city council fundraiser might look something like this:

You are cordially invited to attend a reception honoring

Planning Commissioner

Jane Smith

Candidate for Shady Tree City Council

Host Committee

Councilman Jack Brown Councilwoman Liz Smith
School Trustee Jane White

Platinum Sponsor
$250.00

Gold Sponsor
$150.00

Bronze Sponsor
$100.00

$25.00 per person

RSVP to Paul DePaul at 714-555-2222
Or e-mail
PaulDePaul@treasurer.com

See Attached Remit envelope for information required by law.

The Ballot

"When a king judges, he carefully weighs all the evidence, distinguishing the bad from the good"

Proverbs 20:8, NLT Bible

Ballot designations

Depending on the state you're running in, you may be given the opportunity to list your occupation under your name. Give this a lot of thought. This can be a very important factor in your race for local office.

There'll be a limit on the number of words you can use. Check with your local elections officer for the requirements in your state.

Businessman, businesswoman, small business owner, engineer and accountant are excellent ballot designations for city council. You can also include a commission title in your designation. For example, businessman, planning commissioner is an excellent ballot designation for a city council race.

Teacher is great ballot designation for a school board seat. However, any occupation that indicates a solid post secondary education will work, such as: engineer, businessman and businesswoman, all still good defaults, though including the word Independent in the title (i.e., local independent businessman) may signify that the person running will be an independent thinker once elected.

Water and sanitation district boards are very similar to city council when it comes to selecting a ballot designation. However, anything that would indicate experience in environmental studies would give an edge. For example, engineer trumps businessman in a race of this type.

The Ground Game

It's Not Just For Football

Your campaign manager

Hopefully, you will have a chief volunteer that can help herd your helpers through the process. Odds are you won't be able to hire a professional and will instead be reliant on a competent friend to assume the campaign manager role.

Ken had the pleasure of working with one such individual on a city council race in Orange County, California. Bruce Tartarian was much more together than the many organizers we've come across.

Bruce was kind enough to provide some pointers to would-be campaign managers:

1. Most everything falls under the old adage: "Plan your work and work your plan."
2. A campaign actually starts two to three years before Election Day. Increase the candidate's visibility on local committees, newspaper columns, etc.;
3. The candidate should take a visible leadership role in some local issue. If one is not available, make one. It's great free name recognition.
4. Hire a campaign consultant early on using the following consultant criteria: 1. Battle experience, 2. Local area contacts, and 3. Complimentary to the candidate's strengths. (e.g., in our case, our candidate already had the mostly liberal revolting locals in his camp but needed exposure to the bulk of the actual voters who were more conservative.)
5. Small, flexible "inner circle" campaign staff. No more than four to six persons who are proven, competent professionals are committed to placing the candidate into office, and willing to make their role a top priority through Election Day. Carefully select the inner circle staff by complimentary skills. Know the criteria before you select the members to create a team firing on all cylinders, and to eliminate conflicting overlap and create accountability (most important).
6. Establish position statement early and stick to it. Keep it simple. Take every opportunity to say the same three things over and over and over again.
7. Don't be distracted by side issues. When confronted, see #4.

Most the voters are not even aware (or care) of the non-critical distractions that can creep into a campaign if you let them.

8. The fundraising leader must be focused, set $$$ goals on a timeline, and take full accountability. (e.g., we dropped the ball here in our candidate's 2006 campaign, which caused internal inefficiencies and a post campaign money shortfall).

9. Walking. Similar to the golf saying, "Run ads for show, Walk for dough," said by Bruce Tatarian. In a small town, it's all about the walking. It's critical to have an organized volunteer leader who gives walkers specific assignments with talking points, and then follows up in a disciplined manner. But even more important is for the Candidate to walk, walk, walk, walk and then walk some more. It's a numbers game. The more house calls made, the more incremental votes. And these votes are two-fors because they're stolen from the competition.

10. Do the math. Purchase the past election data and completely understand the voting demographics by precinct. Prioritize precincts as a guide for the walkers and the candidate.

11. Active day-to-day overall campaign manager. Set clear schedules and constantly communicate with other staff leaders.

Precinct operation

A simple yet well executed precinct operation can make up for a lack of financial resources. Your precinct operation needs only to consist of the following to give you an edge:

1. Precinct walks
2. Neighborhood coffees

Everything in war is very simple, but the simplest thing is difficult. The difficulties accumulate and end by producing a kind of friction that is inconceivable unless one has experienced war. Friction is the only concept that more or less corresponds to the factors that distinguish real war from war on paper.[2]

Your campaign is no different.

Nobody is a better salesperson for the candidate than the candidate themself. That is unless they're crazy or have a tendency to drool. Second best is the candidate's spouse, and third are their children. After that come the

---

1   —Clauswitz, Karl von. *On War.* 1832

volunteers.

You need to purchase walk sheets from a reputable vendor. The walk sheets will be broken down by precinct. They will give you the names of those registered to vote in the household, their political affiliation, and frequency of voting. Most voters will also let you know if they prefer to vote absentee or at the polls.

Sometimes you will see two families registered at the same home. Most likely one family moved and another registered at that residence. The data mining isn't able to determine which family resides there now.

Each precinct is broken down into odd and even number addresses.

Select your best precincts based on frequency of voting, density of registration or political affiliation. Buy some clipboards and place each precinct broken down by odd or even number addresses on a single clipboard. Keep the sheets stapled together so they don't fall loose when walking. This way one volunteer can walk one side of the street while another walks down the other side. This will save a lot of time.

Buy a Thomas Guide and copy the precinct to be walked from the Thomas Guide. Purchase some laminate and use it to secure the map on the backside of the clipboard.

Purchase some inexpensive canvas tote bags, the kind used by the environmentally conscious to carry their groceries home from the store. These make excellent totes for carrying your campaign literature.

Ideally, you will want to pair up your volunteers. One will manage the walk sheet and the other will handle campaign material.

Try not to leave the literature loose to blow away. Most people have a welcome mat you can slide the corner of the literature under to help secure it in the event of wind.

You don't want your volunteers to spend too much time at any one door. It wastes time and allows them more time to find an issue to argue about with the voter. A well meaning volunteer can cost you a vote by engaging the voter in a discussion about guns, abortion, presidential politics or any other contentious issue.

You can help minimize time wasting by providing volunteers with a sample script, such as: "Hi, I'm walking for John Smith. He's running for city council. I hope he can earn your vote." Instruct them to hand the literature off, with a "thank you" and then walk away.

Most people will take the literature and tell you they will look at it before shutting the door.

Some people might be too shy to knock on doors. Don't worry. Allow them to leave the material at the door. This is often referred to as a literature or lit drop. At least the material is distributed.

Lit drops most often occur near the end of a race when you want to distribute all your leftover material before the election. Lit drops are time efficient.

Another neat trick is to take a pad of *Post It Notes* and write with a blue sharpie: "Sorry I missed you," and sign: "John" or whatever the candidate's name is. Volunteers can help to write these but make sure someone with similar handwriting does the writing.

Place the note on the literature dropped off at the homes where no one opens the door. The resident will think the candidate came by. This will provide a better impact on the voter.

One of the most important things you can do is treat your volunteers well. You want them to continue coming back and aiding in your precinct walks. This means providing refreshments and healthy doses of praise.

Neighborhood coffee

Select a precinct with a high number of regular voters. We call this high propensity or hi-pro. Pick a precinct that voted in the last three of five elections, for example.

You have supporters in that precinct host their neighbors for coffee and cookies at a place where potential voters will get to meet and talk with you, the candidate.

You can get the address off the walk sheets you purchased. Print or make your own letterhead and address them at the kitchen table.

You don't need a big turn out. The point is to convey your interest in what voters have to say. You just want the voters to receive the letter. It serves as a mailer to that precinct.

Think of these as "friendraisers" instead of a fundraisers.

Your local grocery store

Don't stand in front of your local market passing out your campaign material. You will make way too much contact with people who aren't registered to vote and don't live in your district.

Your time is better spent walking precincts. This way you will know you're contacting actual voters.

Campaign Tangibles

Resist The Urge

Content

Resist the urge to include your entire life story in every piece you print. Odds are you aren't that interesting. Too many candidates load up their brochures and campaign literature with their life story, thoughts on every issue, and photos that weren't good enough to make into the family photo album.

Most voters will look at your campaign literature for about five seconds before they throw it in the trash. Oh yes, no doubt you've gazed at your campaign material with almost a religious reverence. The rest of us just aren't that interested.

First, find someone with a good camera who knows how to take pictures. Most shots should be of your torso up. Full body shots probably put you too far away.

Feel free to stage your photos. During a photo shoot tell your photographer to "think photojournalism." You want action shots to be just that—action shots of you talking to someone, looking like you are doing something.

Voters need to have a clear shot of your face. This might sound obvious but a piece produced by a congressional candidate who spent a quarter of a million dollars on his race showed the back of his head and instead highlighted the person he was speaking to.

Get these basic photos:
- A nice "headshot"
- Photo of you speaking with someone at their door
- Family photo (dog optional)
- Photo with a firefighter or police officer
- Photo with senior citizens
- Photo of you serving the community, if applicable (e.g., if you are on the PTA, have some pictures taken of yourself working the bake sale).

Keep text to a minimum. People don't like to read a wordy document. This will allow you to use a larger font for text. Larger font is easier on the eyes, especially for seniors who comprise the majority of voters.

Keep the message simple. Don't load each piece with too many subjects. You're advertising a product, and you are the product. Look at print advertising. How much information do you see for anything other than a drug ad? Not that much.

Your goal is to persuade voters that you're the best candidate. Your mail needs to appeal to every voter. Don't assume that a voter gets "it," whatever "it" is.

Your message can be emotional to appeal to a voter's sense of reason. Crime, for instance, tends to be an emotional appeal, while jobs and the economy tend to appeal to reason.

Just like advertising; you want to position yourself as the candidate needed to "fight crime," "improve schools," or represent a particular need.

A city councilmember in a L.A. County city centered his campaign on the need for more crossing guards at local schools. This happened to be a big issue in his community that year. All his mail was centered around crossing guards. He found himself referred to as the "crossing guard guy". He won.

Use the language of the voter in your communications. One voter may have a graduate degree in engineering who likes to read technical manuals in bed, while the rest of your potential voters follow a different profile. Most people like to read for entertainment, often two to four grade levels below their actual education. Bearing this in mind, it is important to keep your message simple.

Black and white photos have been relegated to "hit pieces" on the opposition, so you can't get away with B&W photos anymore. People want polished campaign material. Better to buy less of a quality product than more of something no one is going to look at. That means stick to four-color photos.

You can go with two-color photos, too, depending on the layout of the piece. For instance, one side can contain a "letter" from you or an endorser. The flip side can represent something simple, such as:

Elect
Billy Jones
Shady Tree City Council
"Because Leadership Counts"

However, these methods are clearly not as effective as a four-color piece. But if you're at the point where you don't have enough money to produce another mailout with a four-color piece, these methods can be a less expensive alternative.

Sometimes, letters from others are effective. If, for instance, you're running to replace a popular retiring incumbent, you can arrange for a letter touting your candidacy. You may also consider a mailer from your wife to women voters.

Size

Some consultants still cling to the tri-fold brochure. However, the tri-fold is the same size as junk mail. Therefore, you might want to opt to print a "flat" two-sided mailer. You'll need to leave a space for the address of the recipient.

The post office has various rates for different sized flats. Check the latest rates. You might be surprised at how large a flat you can mail for the same cost as a letter.

A printer with political mailer experience should know what the cost to mail is for different size pieces and can advise you accordingly.

Slate mailers

Slate mailers contain a "slate" of candidates on a single mailer. Some slates are good and others aren't. A lot of it has to do with the name of the slate and the universe it is to be mailed to.

The intent of a slate mailer is to convince voters you're the fill-in-the-blank candidate because you're on the hip sounding slate mailer. Most voters don't know candidates pay to be on these slate-style mailers.

Odds are you aren't going to get on the preferred slates unless you're politically connected. That said, you might receive many calls from slate promoters trying to persuade you to buy a spot.

Slates typically run five to ten cents per household, less than a mailer. Of course, you're sharing your information with other candidates.

There is one major downside to lesser-known slates: Do slates actually get mailed to the number of households quoted on the invoice?

Better-known slate mailer consultants will send you a copy of the postal invoice after the race. Lesser-known or less respected slate consultants may have to cut down their mailing universe to save money.

You might receive calls from lesser-known slates that will quote a price. A few weeks later they'll call back with a lower price. Be weary of wasting your time and money on lesser-known slates.

Your budget will determine the number, if any, of slates you do opt to buy. We recommend you add slates as part of your strategy. Avoid making it all your mail budget if at all possible.

Vendors

Printing is an extremely competitive business. You can find a cheap printer, a fast printer and a good printer. Truthfully, you can find fast and good. These are the printers who do the lion's share of political printing. They just don't work cheap.

Your direct mail program (even if what you print is never mailed but walked) is the one thing you shouldn't pinch pennies on because this is how you are going to communicate with voters.

Experienced print and mail houses can actually save you money. Some mail houses specialize in political mail. They are much less likely to make an error in your mail universe. We will touch on this in our discussion on targeting.

Candidates invariably have a friend who is a printer, which is great. Let them make your walk pieces or other print jobs that won't hold your campaign in the balance. What are you going to do if your friend makes an error and doesn't get your mail out? This happens all the time.

There was a good candidate who spent roughly three times the amount of his competition but came in near last. Why? Not only was his material poor quality but also it didn't make it to the post office in time. Voters received the literature he sent the day of the election and for a couple of days after. He used a friend who didn't understand political mail.

A seasoned campaign printer can help you determine the best "drop days." These are the days your mail will be taken to the post office.

Remember, although the post office is supposed to make campaign mail a priority, you're reliant on the individual postal carrier who might take their time depending on the amount of campaign mail they are forced to deliver that election.

Signs

Signs are often a waste of money. Heresy you say? *But everyone has signs. Signs have been a political staple for years.* However, their impact has ebbed significantly. But, if you're going to insist on signage, here's some advice.

First, don't overdo it. The competition, landowners, teenagers walking by and others will tear many of your signs down. You'll find sign destruction a personal insult because you paid for these signs and they have your name on them. But, move on.

Corrugated plastic signs have a better appearance and make better yard signs. Plastic signs are easy to assemble with wire stands much easier placed in yards.

You can probably find a sign company that'll post and take down your signs if you live in an urban area. They generally do a good job because they have "cherry pickers" who can place your signs just out of reach to prevent them from being torn down.

Avoid paper signs unless ordered from a professional sign posting company. Paper signs need to be weather resistant. Many printers do not have the ability to create quality paper signs.

The professional sign posting companies will use a high quality weather resistant paper.

Also, keep your sign message simple. Your name and the office you're running for is plenty of information. Some candidates try to use clever statements on their signs and in so doing are forced to reduce the size of the font. Drivers won't be able to make out anything on a sign with reduced font, least not the candidate's name. A sign is definitely a waste of time and money if those driving past cannot read what it has to say.

Make your name big even if you have to make the office you're running for smaller. Your goal is to reinforce name branding. Ignore the desire to place your photo on any sign. This will not garner you one vote and decreases visibility of your name, which is all voters see on a ballot.

Signs have one purpose and that is to keep your supporters from asking you where your signs are!

California State Assemblyman Tony Strickland (ret.) was able to pull a "gotcha" on his first primary opponent over signs.

He had videotape of his opponent tearing down his signs. Instead, of going to the media with evidence of a "crime" no one really cared about he called a press conference to accuse his opponent of the deed.

Of course, his opponent denied tearing down the signs. Strickland then produced the tape. The press ate it up. We are talking the Los Angeles media market. It's tough to get their attention. They didn't care about the theft. They cared about a frontrunner for State Assembly lying.

Website

Every candidate wants a website because a website can be a valuable tool for those running for legislative offices and races in major cities. Websites provide invaluable information for supporters intending to conduct independent expenditures. But odds are this won't happen in a local race.

Just about the only people who are going to look at your website are your supporters and your opposition. Most voters aren't going to take the time to look at a school board candidate's website.

But should you elect to have one, the same advice provided for campaign material applies to your website. Use a nice large photo of yourself with some basic positions. Don't overdo it. Keep it simple and clean in appearance.

Many web designers like to build in lots of bells and whistles because that is what impresses them. Web designers are not normal people. Most of us can't even figure out how to use all the features on our cell phones.

Intuit is one of the premier tax software companies in the world. They have a division dedicated to simplifying what their software engineers create so regular people can be productive with their product. Keep your website simple and your message will be clear and concise.

Campaign doodads

Someone might ask you for a campaign button, pen or some other doodad. Don't go out and buy them. You will invariably spend money that can be better spent on getting one more piece of mail out.

Many candidates waste money on *campaign doodads*. They think it's neat to have their name on something. Then they run short on important campaign dollars needed during the last stretch of the race. You can pay for buttons when you run for Governor.

Endorsements—which ones to seek

There are some very important endorsements to seek that could lead to other endorsements, volunteers, money and votes. Here are some key endorsements to pursue:

1. Law Enforcement Organizations—Many municipalities will have a Police Officer's Association and a Fire Association. These Associations will help you by donating money, adding credence to your candidacy, and sometimes will even include walkers. They are also great to feature on a mail piece.

2. Elected Officials—You will want to go after elected officials at all levels (Federal, State and Municipal). When getting their endorsement you may want to get a quote to use in your mail pieces and a photo with the elected official. *Note: Only do this with elected officials that are non controversial and not embroiled in any scandals.*

31

3. Prominent Community Members—This would include PTA Presidents, Rotary Presidents, Chamber Board Members, etc. These should be people that others will recognize as responsible, well-known representatives of the community.

Phones—live or recorded

Live calls

You may have some volunteers who cannot walk precincts because of physical limitations or time constraints. A great activity that benefits your campaign is live phone calls. Your data vendor will give you a phone list of donors in the area, and you should provide them with a simple script, such as: *"Hi, this is (insert your own name). I am calling on behalf of my friend and future (insert office name). It is very important to our neighborhood that we have a representative who is (insert key issues here, i.e. a tax fighter, focused on economic revitalization, keeping our streets safe). Can we count on your support?"*

If the answer is yes, attempt to see if you can get them an absentee ballot application (via e-mail or fax).

If the answer is no, thank them and terminate the call.

If the answer is maybe, attempt to sell them on the virtues of your candidate. See if there are any issues you can help them with.

Recorded calls

Your first thought may be *"I hate those annoying recorded calls,"* but the truth is, while you may hate them, recorded calls are a great way to build name brand ID. Often, it is great to use a well-known endorser to record the call (i.e., a popular mayor, members of the law enforcement community, etc.). Your script may sound something like this: *"Hi this is [Lieutenant XXX] from the Police Department. As you may know, Tuesday is Election Day, and it is imperative that we support candidate [XXX]. [XXX] will be the candidate we can trust to keep our streets safe and our children secure. On Tuesday please join me in voting for [XXX]."*

Your Audience

Know how to pick them

This might sound obvious but you don't want to mail to citizens who can't or won't vote. There are data mining vendors who will sell you this type of information for roughly one to two cents per name. Contact your local political party for a list of vendors in your area.

You will probably want to mail to voters who have voted in the last three out of five elections. The data mining company will e-mail a target list to the printer's mail house. These names should be "householded." This way only one piece will be mailed to each home.

This is where experience with campaign mail is important. Those unfamiliar with political mail campaigns might send your campaign mail to each voter. That means one home might receive four pieces. This is a huge waste.

Experience enables you to target your message. For instance, a message for seniors can be mailed to those 55 and over. You can also alter your message for the political party of the voter you are communicating with. The data mining company can sort this mailing universe for you.

Bear in mind that printing costs will decrease by the size of the print job. You might not be able to afford a certain kind of segmentation.

This is how it is supposed to work: You pick a reputable political mail printer. You provide their graphics person with what you want printed. They put together a proof for approval.

Your data mining company sends your political mail printer a voter list. This list will let you know how many mail pieces you will need. Printing is then rounded off so you will have extras you can walk. You might want the printer to print some extras above that to decrease the cost of your walk pieces.

The printer will label the mail and deliver it to the mail house. You will need to provide money for postage to the mail house. The mail house will deliver the mailer to the post office.

The data mining company can let you know who is likely to vote by absentee ballot and who is likely to vote on the day of the election. Don't print the same material twice. Print enough to cover both voting universes and have them delivered to the post office in two drops. For example:

- There are 10,000 hi-propensity voters

- 4000 vote absentee and 7,000 vote the day of the election

- You print 10,000 pieces; 4000 are taken to the post office the same day absentee ballots are mailed out by the registrar of voters

- The other 7000 are mailed during the last two weeks of the race

Polling

Do you really know?

Polling

One of our favorite pollsters is Adam Probolsky, Chairman & CEO of Probolsky Research, LLC. He offered some thoughts on polling.

Probolsky says every campaign, whether for water board, mayor, state legislature, governor or president can benefit from voter opinion research polling. A good pollster is one that has a demonstrated track record of predicting outcomes. Hire one of those.

He also notes there are numerous reasons to poll, not just to know if you are winning or not, but also to test messages, help target your resources and get positive press.

Before election season even starts

When you begin to think about running for office or even re-election a poll can be a helpful tool, even if you don't know who your opponent(s) will be.

Two of the most important elements to a campaign are decided the day you file to run. The candidate's ballot title and ballot statement (if allowed for the office) may be the only communication a voter sees from your campaign. So choose your words wisely.

In California there is a whole set of rules about what three words you are allowed to use, but I always prefer something that sounds like an official position. If you sit on several boards and commissions or can choose between businesswoman and parent and planning commissioner and community volunteer, its best to poll them and see which is more attractive to the voters in your community.

The same goes for ballot statements. This is your chance to reach every voting household with a message from you. Make it impactful and be sure to speak to the issues that the voters care about. If you are running for city council and you are excited about parks and trails but the voters want their city council members to focus on traffic congestion relief, you may miss the mark. Polling not only allows you to test how voters feel about your issues, but polling also helps you identify what is tops on their minds.

Polling can help with fund raising, too. Aside from close personal friends and family, donors like to bet on winners. So if you can demonstrate that an early poll gives you a leg up, use it. Promote it. Get your pollster or consultant to write a memo on the results and fax, mail and e-mail results to the donor community. This will make fund raising calls go much better and attract donors you never knew existed.

Likewise, local media especially is always looking for a good story. If the results are good and your campaign strategist thinks there is value in getting a story out there, share some of the data with the press. They generally eat up polling results, and like donors, the American people like to support winners, too.

Getting geared up

Once you know your competition, and hopefully know their strengths and weaknesses, as well as the same for you, poll it collectively. Poll you and your opponent's (s') positive background information such as service on a hospital board or education board, and include negatives such as bankruptcies or lawsuits. The goal is to see what sticks. Positive and negative. You may be very proud of your master's degree in international relations, but voters might be much more interested in your decade long involvement with the local PTA.

Likewise, there may be a certain demographic (say all Republicans and men between 25 and 65) down on your opponent for his support of rent control, while another demographic (chiefly, Democrats) who view your opponent more favorably knowing they support rent control. This is where targeting comes in. A mail piece that reaches your opponent on rent control will go only to those households where the demographic meets the profile gleaned from the poll that would respond well to that particular message.

This type of targeting will be repeated over and over again for community forums and direct mail and phone calls, and for walk pieces.

In the heat of the battle

It's two weeks before the election and you think you're on the right track; you're receiving positive feedback from voters calling your headquarters and from walking door-to-door, but bear in mind you never know for sure until you poll. Polling at this late stage helps give the candidate, and oftentimes the spouse of the candidate, some hope or peace of mind. But, forget that—just keep working as if you are losing by one vote.

The real benefits of polling at this time are to test for accuracy and effect. Early polling helps you shape your message and define your campaign. Late polling helps you understand if you are on target and if you need to modify the message or counter a message being proffered by your opponent(s). Plus polling can provide you some peace of mind.

There is often a temptation to track the polling all the way to Election Day; we call this a rolling track, which can be done for any length of time, for instance the 10 days preceding the election. It's fun to watch and if you have the resources to do something with the information, such as send one or two last pieces of mail out, or make a few rounds of phone calls, or place paid or volunteer walkers in the precincts, rolling tracks are very helpful. However, if you are low on funds and you decide to track rather than dedicate precious resources to voter communication, you are making a mistake.

Negative Campaigning

What it is and how we do it

When to use negative campaigning

Some people will say go heavy with "hit pieces" against your opponent. Others will tell you only to speak positive. Both schemes are correct in certain instances.

Sometimes candidates will have a knee-jerk reaction and go negative right out of the gate. This is usually a mistake because sometimes your opponent doesn't have enough money to campaign, and by choosing the negative, all you're going to accomplish is to give them credibility and free advertising by alerting more voters about your opponent.

Many candidates only want to run a positive campaign. They believe voters are "sick" of negative campaigning. Though voters do say they don't like negative campaigning, voters still respond to negative messages.

That said, just what is negative campaigning? What does negative messaging really mean? It's a clever way to pinpoint your opponent's downfalls. Now, it's easy to overdo it and hit your opponent too hard below the belt, and since voters don't respond well to this kind of messaging, it's best to be subtle. For instance, draw contrasts between you and your opponent based on past votes and stated positions. Point out the lack of a record or what can't be perceived as an error made on your opponent's part.

Humor is a good way to couch your hit. If at all possible, your mail should be clever. Writing a negative piece is much more challenging than producing fluff.

What to go negative on

There are some things to search for when looking for negative items about your opponent, such as:

1. Tax Liens—these are very easy to research. Visit your local county court house and ask for assistance. Tax liens are a great thing to go negative on because they prove that your opponent has no respect for rules and is irresponsible.

2. Bankruptcies—these are also very easy to research. Again, visit your local county court house and ask for assistance. Bankruptcies are great to show that your opponent has no responsibility when it comes to finances.

3. City Council Minutes—these are more time consuming to research. To find minutes, visit your city clerk's office, or go online and search

for an archive of minutes. You'll want to search for irresponsible votes, including fee raises, tax raises and pay raises.

Don't be afraid to point out a legitimate chink in your opponent's armor. It's much easier to be a good winner then a good loser.

However, don't waste your money going negative on someone who isn't running a decent campaign. You will only be providing them name identification they couldn't afford to buy themselves.

Weeds

Don't let them get you down

The city of two hundred

Most every community has a core group of people who are involved in most everything. They usually belong to multiple organizations and think of themselves as "opinion leaders." You might even find many of them don't even live in the district you are running in.

Your ability to get elected rarely has anything to do with whether or not these people support you, but they will make you feel good or bad for every little thing that happens. The larger the community you are running in the less they matter. Don't get caught up in playing to them. Instead, focus on the voters.

Blogs

Your community might also have a blog presence to consider. Some blogs are nothing more than adult graffiti while others are frequented heavily by insiders. Much of blog's utility depends on the blog's administrator.

Don't ruminate too much about what is on your local political blogs. Give them an appropriate amount of attention. Blogs popular among the political insiders can be a useful way to disseminate information quickly. They can also be used to create early momentum among activists and some donors.

The Local Party

If used right, can be one of your greatest assets

Endorsements

Most counties have a mechanism built into their central county committees that enables the county party to endorse a candidate in a municipal election. Sometimes endorsements are decided upon unilaterally by the Chairman of the Committee, and sometimes they are decided on by a sub-group of the Central Committee (an endorsement committee or selection group).

If your county is one that allows endorsements, you should seek them with a vengeance. Especially if you are a first time candidate, alerting potential voters to this when precinct walking, debating, or highlighting the party in a mail piece adds a "stamp of approval" and a sense that you have been screened and are acceptable.

What to expect from an endorsement committee

Endorsement committees will want to know that your core beliefs are in line with what the party believes. They may ask you to fill out a questionnaire or question you in person. Do your research! Make sure that you do not sabotage your own endorsement because you didn't find out what the party platform is and thus ended up making statements that were viewed as hostile.

Remember, after you get elected to your first office, people may start to think of you as a candidate for future higher office. Many committees will look at this early endorsement request as their opportunity to be the gatekeepers for your political future.

Volunteers

Your county party is a great resource for volunteers. Remember that the county party keeps a database of all people in a region who have expressed interest in past and current elections of displaying a yard sign, phone banking, walking precincts, and/or hosting coffees.

If you are running during the same time as a Presidential, Senate or Gubernatorial campaign is occurring, the county party will already be immersed in volunteer activities in your municipality. Ask the chairman if volunteers can also pass out your materials when precinct walking, display your yard signs in addition to the top-ticket candidate, and if they could mention your name when phone banking. If you are running in an off year, you can ask your chairman for the list of volunteers and make calls through them to get people involved in your race.

Slates

Many local parties will already have reserved slates and they may ask you to pick up a partial fee or reimburse them for what they have already paid for. Oftentimes, you will save money if the party has already reserved a spot on the slate. Parties have done this for many candidates because it gives them a bulk discount.

Fundraising

Central committee leaders traditionally know some of the top donors in the region, and many have close, pre-existing, working relationships with donors. Ask these committee leaders who they know, and the appropriateness of making an introduction for you over lunch, coffee or the phone.

Also, many central committees have money earmarked for local campaigns. Check with your chairperson to find out if your committee is one of these, and find out what you need to do to be considered for a donation.

Member Communications

In some areas, where there are campaign limits, you will find your financial resources somewhat tight. County parties have the opportunity to communicate to members (people of that party registered to vote) without any limits. Not only is a connection to members an effective way to create more mailouts and phone calls, but also a notice coming from the "Official Party" is considered professional sounding.

Data

As discussed earlier, data is key to your race. In more sophisticated counties, data is provided free of charge.

Once Elected

Stay engaged and re-election will be easier

Rule of thumb

Generally, staying in office requires the officeholder to provide quality representation. Of course there are circumstances when an elected official becomes corrupt, incompetent or any combination thereof. These folks will often garner lots of earned media detailing their various exploits. Don't become one of them.

Continue to raise money

Sometimes, after a candidate wins, they think it's time for a fundraising holiday until their next campaign. This is a huge mistake. If as an elected official, you succeed, your goal is to hold a fundraiser annually while you're in office to make the amount you have to raise less when election time rolls around.

Make friends with those who opposed you

The knee-jerk reaction after a campaign is: Never make friends with your opponent, and: Distance yourself from their supporters. Actually, you should do the complete opposite. Reach out to both opponents and their supporters, become their friend and watch as they become converts into your camp for your next election.

Endorse smartly and selectively

Many people will come to you from neighboring districts and overlapping regions seeking your endorsement. Be careful. The person who gives an endorsement too often makes it irrelevant, and likewise, the person who endorses a losing candidate sometimes suffers repercussions from a bad endorsement. On the positive side, if the candidate you endorsed wins, you have a lifelong ally.

Media relations

Two rules you should always remember when speaking with the media:
  1. Don't lie.
  2. Stay on message

Chances are you aren't running for an office that is going to attract an incredible amount of media attention, such as races run in rural communities, which tend to be covered by local media, much more so than races run in urban areas.

Back to the basic rules. You want to establish yourself as a credible individual. Don't develop a reputation for being less than honest. It can haunt you for a very long time and render you a target for negative attention from the media.

Reporters might be writing a story on any number of issues revolving around the race and your candidacy. Your responses should be consistent with your theme.

You should stick to a basic theme to promote in your campaign. Stay on message when during interviews about the race.

You also need to stick to speaking on the issues you're campaigning on. This is your message.

There may be times when you will want to issue a press release. Again, your community will dictate the likelihood of your press release getting picked up by the press or printed in a local paper.

Press releases have standard formats, such as:

Citizens for Jane Smith	Contact: Jack Smith
1234 Elm Street 5	55-5555
Smalltown, USA	

For Immediate Release
Smith Outpaces Opponents in Fundraising

Smalltown—Jane Smith announced today she has raised more money in the last reporting period than all her opponents. "Jane is clearly the front runner in this race," said her campaign manager, Jack Smith.

Community leaders are rallying behind Jane. Smalltown Council members Jones and McCoy and many other local leaders endorse her.

"Jane Smith is a dynamic candidate and will be a great asset to this community," said Councilmember Jones.

#   #   #

Obviously, your press release will be longer than the above sample. You need to make your lead sentence important. Get to the point. The media receives countless releases. You want yours to stand out. Just don't overdo it. Be professional.

Odds are press calls will either be fielded by the candidate, the candidate's spouse or campaign manager. If someone other than the candidate takes the call, have them inquire of the reporter what the subject of the discussion will be and when is the reporter's deadline. This will give you time to think about messaging. Being responsive to the reporter's deadline will help to make you a more likely contact for the media.

Lastly, avoid speaking off the record. You want to be a public figure. You should want to be on the record. Let others provide background material.

Final Thoughts

Being a successful candidate generally requires you to gather resources, recruit volunteers, develop a winning message and be committed to victory. You need to be focused. You should have a severe disinterest in those persons who can't vote for you and won't be giving you money.

Neophytes to politics might find this a harsh perspective. "I want to talk to everybody and hear what they have to say," said one losing candidate. Losing here the operative word.

For example, a very contentious school board race was taking place in a very large district. There were allegations of corruption that ultimately led to some indictments by the District Attorney. A forum was organized by the PTA and the League of Women Voters. No visual media was going to be present.

The challengers I (Ken) was advising inquired as to whether they should go to a forum they believed to be pre-disposed to favoring the incumbents. They were advised not to waste their time. Instead, they went to a high school football game in the district and distributed their materials at the gate.

Typically, I don't recommend this type of haphazard voter contact but parents who attend school sporting events are most likely concerned with their school boards.

I attended the forum. Questions from the audience were requested. I submitted several questions myself dealing with many of the issues that were featured in news stories appearing in the county's paper of record. I was hoping to receive some useful statements from incumbents that could be used against them.

The League of Women Voters selected none of the questions I submitted. Instead, the questions were limited to fairly benign issues. You'd have no idea there were any problems in the district based on the questions posed to the candidates.

Conventional thinking among the uninitiated would be to attend the forum. The winning strategy was to engage voters.

The candidates who don't win are often referred to as "also-rans." Their names aren't typically remembered.

Lastly, winning requires hard work. You can make up for a lack of funds with a healthy dose of perspiration. Your ability to win will depend largely on your personal commitment to victory.

About the Authors

Ken Maddox is President of Orange County-based public policy and communications strategy consulting firm Maddox Government Relations. He is also Director of Legislative Affairs for California Board of Equalization Member, Michelle Steel.

He has served as a consultant on many winning campaigns ranging from local school boards to statewide elected offices.

The Vietnamese American Broadcasters Association has recognized Ken for his success in the Vietnamese-American media market.

As a former Garden Grove City councilman, he was elected to represent Central Orange County in the California State Assembly where he served from 1998 to 2004.

Ken also served as past vice president of Republicans for Environmental Protection, California Chapter.

While in the legislature, he served on a variety of policy committees that include insurance, utilities and commerce, governmental organization, environmental safety and toxics, agriculture, education and local government.

Once a volunteer firefighter, he attended the Los Angeles County Sheriff's Academy and worked for two years as deputy sheriff. He then served 15 years as a police officer with the City of Tustin.

Ken is a past member of the Board of Directors for Breast Cancer Survivors and is also a volunteer for his church.

He served in the Army National Guard from 1981 to 1989 and received a commission as second lieutenant in 1984. After September 11, 2001, Ken rejoined the California Army National Guard. The Governor awarded him the Order of California, the highest award presented to a civilian or member of the military by the California National Guard for his service to our country and on behalf of veterans.

Ken earned a Bachelor of Science degree in Communication Arts from California State Polytechnic at Pomona, and a Master of Arts degree in Management from National University. He was a senior fellow in UCLA's

School of Public Policy and Social Research for the 2004/2005 session.

Ken and his son reside in Orange County, California.

Michael Richman is a longtime political leader and consultant of California politics. In March 2004, he was named campaign manager of the Greg Hill for State Assembly Campaign (CA-53). During his tenure in that position, Michael was named MVP Campaign Manager by Calraces, an Insider's Commentary on California Politics.

From 2004 to 2007, Johnson-Clark Associates employed Michael; while there, he was involved with municipal, legislative, supervisory and statewide constitutional campaigns. During the last cycle, Michael served as deputy campaign manager for Insurance Commissioner Steve Poizner, and campaign manager to Board of Equalization member Michelle Steel. He was also involved in more than 14 winning campaigns across California.

Recently, Capitol Weekly Newspapers named him as one of 30 up-and-comers in California politics. Michael won the 2007 American Association of Political Consultants National Rookie of the Year award.

Michael got his start in politics in 1998 while working in the field office of Randy Hoffman for Congress.

During 2001, Michael worked for Steve Soboroff for the Los Angeles Mayor Campaign; he also served as congressional page under Deputy Whip Eric Cantor (R-VA).

Michael then went on to serve as an assistant producer for the Al Rantel Show, where he conducted screenings, guest bookings, and researched and produced topic development.

During 2003, Michael worked directly under the executive director of the Republican Jewish Coalition, where he helped the Southern California region grow to more than 1,000 members. He is also the former executive director of the San Bernardino county Republican party.

Michael is a graduate of the University of Southern California Annenberg's School of Communications. He lives in Sherman Oaks, California, where he enjoys reading, and rooting for his beloved New York Yankees and USC Trojans.